Hyenas

By Ethan Grucella

Gareth Stevens
Publishing

Please visit our Web site, www.garethstevens.com. For a free color catalog of all our high-quality books, call toll free 1-800-542-2595 or fax 1-877-542-2596.

Library of Congress Cataloging-in-Publication Data

Grucella, Ethan.
 Hyenas / Ethan Grucella.
    p. cm. – (Animals that live in the grasslands)
Includes index.
ISBN 978-1-4339-3870-2 (pbk.)
ISBN 978-1-4339-3871-9 (6-pack)
ISBN 978-1-4339-3869-6 (library binding)
1. Hyenas–Juvenile literature. I. Title.
QL737.C24G78 2011
599.74'3–dc22

                                            2010008463

First Edition

Published in 2011 by
Gareth Stevens Publishing
111 East 14th Street, Suite 349
New York, NY 10003

Copyright © 2011 Gareth Stevens Publishing

Designer: Michael J. Flynn
Editor: Therese Shea

Photo credits: Cover, pp. 1, 5, 7 (all), 9, 11, 13, 17, 19, 21, back cover Shutterstock.com; p. 15 DEA/F. Galardi/De Agostini/Getty Images.

Printed in the United States of America

CPSIA compliance information: Batch #CS10GS: For further information contact Gareth Stevens, New York, New York at 1-800-542-2595.

Table of Contents

Boldface words appear in the glossary.

What's So Funny?

Have you ever wondered why a hyena "laughs"? It is telling other hyenas that it has found food. These deadly animals live in the **grasslands** of Asia and Africa.

There are three kinds of hyenas. Spotted hyenas are famous for "laughing." They are the largest kind. There are also striped hyenas and brown hyenas.

striped hyena

brown hyena

spotted hyena

Built for the Hunt

A hyena is built to hunt. It has long front legs to run fast. It has thick **muscles** in its neck, shoulders, and jaws. These muscles help it carry and eat other animals.

thick neck

long legs

9

Hyenas can see, hear, and smell very well. They hunt mostly at night. Hyenas eat a lot at one time. They may not eat again for a few days.

Hyenas eat young hippos, zebras, **wildebeests**, plants, and fish. Hyenas also eat dead animals, bones, and even animal droppings!

Clans

A group of hyenas is called a clan. Each clan marks its land with its smell. This tells other clans not to hunt there.

clan

Hyenas in a clan may work together to kill an animal. **Female** spotted hyenas lead their clan. They are bigger than the **males**. Females give the best meat to their cubs.

cub

Hyenas may travel many miles each day to find food. When they find it, they "talk" to each other. Their screams and laughs can be heard miles away.

Hyena Hunters

People hunt hyenas to keep their animals safe. Many hyenas have been killed. To make sure they do not all disappear, they are **protected** in some places.

Fast Facts

Height	up to 35 inches (89 centimeters)
Length	up to 59 inches (150 centimeters) from head to rear; tail is up to 14 inches (36 centimeters)
Weight	up to 190 pounds (85 kilograms)
Diet	animals, plants, fish, dead animals, and animal droppings
Average life span	up to 25 years in the wild

Glossary

female: a girl

grasslands: land on which grass is the main kind of plant life

male: a boy

muscle: a part of the body that helps other parts move

protect: to guard from harm

wildebeest: a large African animal with a mane, beard, horns, and tail

For More Information

Books

Malam, John. *Hyenas.* New York, NY: Franklin Watts, 2008.

Markle, Sandra. *Hyenas.* Minneapolis, MN: Lerner Publications Company, 2005.

Web Sites

Hyena

www.awf.org/content/wildlife/detail/hyena
Read about the life of a hyena. Also watch a video of a spotted hyena in action.

Spotted Hyena

animals.nationalgeographic.com/animals/mammals/hyena.html
Find more facts about the spotted hyena as well as pictures and a map.

Index

About the Author

Though a practicing physician like his parents, Ethan Grucella is an amateur zoologist with an enthusiasm for African animals. He lives in Cleveland, Ohio, where he writes wildlife books in his spare time.